GETTING TO THE 750!!

The Credit Score Game Revealed

By

Nadia Triplett

Copyright © 2021

ISBN 9798549447486

Table of Contents

Introduction

One of the leading causes of financial stress many American consumers face is associated with the lack of credit or bad credit. A lower credit score minimizes buying power and demonstrates greater risk to lenders. In some cases, long-term financial impacts of credit denial and hardships lead to mental and physical conditions because of limited resources, otherwise afforded to others with a higher credit score.

The goal of this book is to provide key strategies of establishing credit, increasing scores and methods used to successfully dispute with Credit Bureaus while applying federal consumer laws.

There are a lot of credit repair companies and debt counseling organizations constantly advertising through various marketing platforms to lure consumers in with expensive repair/restoration packages when the process can be completed without wasting tons of money through education and self-monitoring of what is reported in your credit file.

As you begin to navigate through each chapter of this book, you will begin to understand the power of using the law and time-tested actions to build credit as well as successful strategies for getting the right results from Credit Bureaus.

CHAPTER 1

Fair Credit Reporting Act

WHAT IS THE PURPOSE OF THE FAIR CREDIT REPORTING ACT?

The Fair Credit Reporting Act (FCRA) is a federal law that regulates how consumer data is collected, accessed, used and reported within credit files. The intent of the law is to protect consumer information from negligent reporting of inaccurate data by credit reporting agencies.

When Congress enacted the Fair Credit Reporting Act (FCRA) in 1970, it was an amendment to 1968

Credit Protection Act to strengthen the data protection laws.

The FCRA outlines specific rules and laws credit reporting agencies, creditors, collection agencies (third-party collectors) and banks must follow when reporting consumer data. They are furnishers of the data and required to do the following actions:

- Report complete and accurate information to credit reporting agencies
- Investigate consumer disputes
- Verify, or delete inaccurate data within 30 days of receipt
- Notify consumers within 5 days of reporting negative information that was previously deleted from their report and will be added back

Ultimately, FCRA outlines consumer rights and guidelines to ensure violations or non-compliant actions are governed accordingly.

CHAPTER 2

Consumer Rights under FCRA

How Does the FCRA Help Consumers?

The FCRA incorporates layers of protection through prescribed regulations to ensure   consumers personal data is used and reported with purposeful intent. Key aspects of the law that provide protection to consumers follows:

- ✔ The FCRA gives consumers rights of notification about information used to deny applications for credit, employment, or insurance.

- ✔ Under the Fair and Accurate Credit Transaction Act (FACTA), which is an amendment to the FCRA, consumers have the right to request and access their file disclosure report. Consumers get one free credit report from each national credit bureau every 12 months, by going to AnnualCreditReport.com.

✔   The FCRA gives consumers the right to access credit reports but restricts access to others unless they have a "permissible purpose," such as landlords, creditors, and insurance companies. If an employer wants to see your credit report, you must give written consent; employers must meet other requirements as well, and not all states allow employers to pull credit reports as part of an applicant's background check. For example, California, Vermont and Nevada have enacted laws that restrict use of credit checks for employment.

✔   The FCRA gives consumers the right to dispute inaccurate, incomplete, missing or unverifiable information listed in credit reports. The credit bureau will perform an investigation by contacting the data furnisher to verify whether the information is accurate. If the information is <u>unverifiable</u>, typically within 30-45 days, the credit bureaus are required to delete it from the consumer report. If results of an investigation determine the information is <u>verified</u>, a consumer reporting agency will continue to report the information and add comments/remarks to your credit file referencing their findings. As a consumer, you have the right to request the <u>method of verification</u>. If the credit bureaus cannot provide <u>sufficient evidence </u>an item belongs to you, the law requires it to be removed from your report. Additionally, <u>accurate negative information</u>, such as bankruptcies and late payments, typically remains on the consumer file for 7 seven years.

✔   The FCRA gives you the option to opt out of prescreened credit offers received.

Finally, the FCRA gives you the ability to put a **security freeze** on your credit report, which prevents potential lenders from checking your credit report without permission. You can provide lenders with a one-time PIN number to access your credit report.

Security freezes prevent a consumer reporting agency from releasing information without express authorization. The security freeze is designed to prevent credit, loans, and services from being approved in your name without consent. However, be aware that using a security freeze to restrict access of personal and financial information could potentially delay, interfere, or prohibit timely approvals of any subsequent request or application submitted regarding a new loan, mortgage, or any other account involving extension of credit.

As an alternative to a security freeze, you have the right to place an initial or extended **fraud alert** on your credit file at no cost. An initial fraud alert is placed on a consumer's credit file for 1 year. When credit lenders access a consumer report that specifies a fraud alert, the lender is required to verify the consumer's identity before extending new credit. If you are a victim of identity theft, you are entitled to an extended fraud alert monitoring service lasting **7 years**.

If you have an existing account with a collection agency—or its affiliates—a security freeze cannot be applied. The account must remain accessible for reviewing and collection activities. Reviewing the account includes activities related to account maintenance, monitoring, credit line increases, account upgrades and enhancements.

By law, if a credit report or another type of consumer report is used to deny an application for credit, insurance, employment or to take another adverse action, consumer notifications are required. The creditor is required to provide the name, address, and phone number of the agency that provided information.

ACCESS CONSUMER DISCLOSURE REPORTS

You have the right to know what is in your file. You may request and obtain all the information in the files of a consumer reporting agency. You will be required to provide proper identification, which may include your social security number. In many cases, the consumer file disclosure will be free. A free disclosure report is permissible under the following circumstances:

- ✔ A person has taken adverse action against you because of information in your credit report;

- ✔ You are the victim of identity theft and place a fraud alert in your file;

- ✔ Your file contains inaccurate information because of fraud;

- ✔ You are on public assistance;

- ✔ You are unemployed but expect to apply for employment within 60 days.

In addition, all consumers are entitled to **one free consumer disclosure report every 12 months** upon request from each nationwide credit bureau and nationwide specialty consumer reporting agencies.

CHAPTER 3

Credit Competency is Key

Why Credit Information Matters

Credit is a huge part of a consumer's financial reputation and impacts virtually every aspect of life. When applying for a credit card, car loan, mortgage loan or any other form of credit, the issuing company checks your credit history to assess creditworthiness. The terms offered by lenders are partially based on your credit score and information in your credit reports.

Credit history affects more than your ability to get loans or the best annual percentage rate **(APR)** on credit cards. For instance, prospective landlords could check credit reports to see how creditworthy you are when assessing your ability to pay rent on time.

In some states, employers may check credit reports for hiring purposes. Also, depending on the state, insurance companies may check credit information to determine whether to offer you coverage at a favorable rate.

The Basics: How Credit Works

Credit reports and scores reflect how well financial responsibilities are managed over a certain period. Maintaining a good credit score broadens opportunities and increases buying power. A few benefits afforded to consumers are:

Obtain credit cards and loans with lower interest rates;

- ✔ Improve your lifestyle through purchases that are only possible with excellent credit;

- ✔ Obtain services with less stress if you have a credit card—like renting a car. (Without a credit card, there could be additional requirements, including a credit inquiry);

- ✔ Have financial resources (line of credit) to pay unexpected emergencies.

However, there are risks involved with credit. Poorly managed credit can result in debt and a challenging recovery process. A good credit history cannot be restored overnight but can be improved with time.

The rules of establishing good credit are simple. A lender extends a line of credit and you agree to pay the lender back the amount spent plus interest charges and perhaps additional service fees. A payment schedule is set up and requires payments according to the agreed terms. Paying according to the agreed terms has the highest weight on credit scores. Through this book, you will see repeated statements, highlighting the importance of paying bills on time because payment history is **35% of your credit score**.

TYPES OF CREDIT

Consumer credit is categorized in four ways:

1. **Revolving credit**: This type of credit is open-ended; when you borrow, you agree to repay a certain amount each month, but you will not be expected to repay all the money by a definite deadline. Instead, you will be able to carry a balance and borrow more—up to a preset limit—each month. The interest

amount paid on a debt is directly impacted by the remaining unpaid principal balance. Credit cards are the most common form of revolving credit. Revolving Utilization will measure the aggregate credit card balances and credit card limits. The utilization percentage is calculated by dividing the total credit card balances by total credit limits and multiplying the result by 100. This percentage is impacted when credit card accounts are closed because it lowers the aggregate limit compared to the balance. Additionally, closing the accounts will lower credit scores in the short run. Credit card companies typically close accounts with no activity for 18 months.

2. **Charge cards**: Charge cards look and work like credit cards, but you must pay the balance in full each month.

3. **Service credit:** Anyone who provides a service and bills in arrears (after the receipt of goods or services) extends service credit to you. This type of credit includes utility

companies, landlords (if you rent an apartment), mobile phone provider, etc. Each month, you pay a fixed amount.

While this kind of credit doesn't typically appear on credit reports, if you fail to pay on time, these creditors could report late payments to credit bureaus or send accounts to a collections agency that reports late payments, causing negative information to appear on credit reports.

4. **Installment credit**: These accounts consist of fixed amount consumers, who agree to pay plus interest over the life of the loan, usually ranging from months to years. Typically, installment loans include origination fees, late fees and other terms that are documented in the agreement. For instance, a mortgage loan includes closing cost, points, and private mortgage insurance if your down payment is less than 20% of the home purchase price.

UNDERSTANDING CREDIT SCORES

No campaign to build credit would be complete without giving some attention to credit scores. Before deciding to approve a loan, creditors will consider your credit score. The first action creditors will take when considering approving you for a loan is checking credit scores.

Credit scores are a **three-digit number** between **300 and 850** lenders use to assess how much risk is involved by extending credit and the probability of prompt repayments. The score is based on information in current credit reports, called **credit score factors**. It is intended to be an objective, reliable way for lenders to assess a borrower's potential creditworthiness. Higher scores make consumers eligible for loans and credit cards with favorable terms.

There are multiple credit reporting agencies and many different credit scoring models produce variations of credit scores. Credit scores are not included in credit reports and a separate request is required to obtain that information. Generally,

FICO and VantageScore® are the most common credit scores in lending decisions.

Information on your credit report that influence scores include:

- **Payment history**
- **Credit utilization ratio**
- **Types of credit**
- **Credit history**
- **Total balances on all debts owe**
- **Public records like bankruptcies**
- **Credit inquiries**

How Credit Scores Are Calculated

You likely have dozens—if not hundreds—of credit scores. That is because a credit score is calculated by applying a mathematical algorithm to information in one of three credit reports, and there is no uniform algorithm employed by all lenders or financial companies to compute scores. Some credit scoring models are common, like the **FICO Score**, which ranges from **300 to 850**.

Do not focus on having multiple scores because factors that make your scores go up or down in different scoring models are usually similar. **"What makes one score go up versus down is always going to be the same—it just depends on the degree," says Barry Paperno**, a consumer credit expert.

Most scoring models consider payment history on loans, credit cards balance, revolving credit usage, credit history, credit mix and how often you apply for new credit.

CHAPTER 4

Strategies for Building Credit Scores

STEPS TO IMPROVE YOUR CREDIT SCORES

To improve credit scores, always pull the current scores from a company such as **myFICO.com**. myFICO provides all 3 credit reports and scores, but it is a little expensive. Another option is **Credit Check Total.** This company provides all 3 credit reports and scores and is owned by Experian. Both companies provide information about major factors affecting your scores. These risk factors will help you understand the changes needed to start improving scores. You will need to allow some time for any changes made to be reported by creditors and subsequently reflected in credit scores.

Of course, certain credit score factors are typically more important than others. Payment history and credit utilization ratios are among the most important in many critical credit scoring models, and together, they can represent up **to 70% of a credit score**, which means they have huge influence.

Focusing on the following actions will help your credit scores improve over time. A credit score reflects credit payment patterns with more emphasis on recent information.

1. Pay Your Bills on Time

When lenders review credit reports and request a credit score, they are interested in how reliably you are paying bills. Past payment performance is usually considered a good predictor of future performance.

You can positively influence this credit scoring factor by paying all your bills on time as agreed every month. Paying late or settling an account for less than originally agreed can negatively affect credit scores.

Pay all bills on time, not just credit card bills, loans, auto loans or student loans, also rent, utilities, phone bills and so on. It is a good idea to use resources and tools available, such as automatic payments or calendar reminders, to ensure timely payments every month.

If you are behind on any payments, update them as soon as possible. Although late or missed payments appear as negative information on credit reports for seven years, the impact on credit scores declines over time. Older late payments have less effect than more recent ones.

2. Get Credit for Making Utility and Cell Phone Payments on Time

Making utility and cell phone payments on time is another way to improve credit scores through a free product called **Boost**.

Through this new opt-in product, consumers can allow Experian to connect to their bank accounts to identify utility and telecom payment history. After a consumer verifies data and confirm they want it added to their Experian credit file, an updated **FICO Score** will be delivered in real time.

3. Pay off Debt and Keep Balances Low on Credit Cards and Other Revolving Credit

The credit utilization ratio is another important number in credit score calculations. It is calculated by adding all your credit card balances at any given time and dividing that amount by your total credit limit. For example, if you typically charge about $2,000 each month and your total credit limit across all your cards is $10,000, your utilization ratio is 20%.

To figure out your average credit utilization ratio, look at all your credit card statements from the last 12 months. Add the statement balances for each month across all your cards and divide by 12. That is how much credit you use on average each month.

Lenders typically like to see low ratios of **30% or less,** and people with the best credit scores often have extremely low credit utilization ratios. A low credit utilization ratio tells lenders you have not maxed out your credit cards and likely know how to manage credit well. You can positively influence your credit utilization ratio by:

- Paying off debt and keeping credit card balances low. **Remember, if you do not use your revolving credit cards every few months, they may not report to the Bureaus!**

- Becoming an authorized user on another person's account (as long as they use credit responsibly). As an authorized user, you have zero liability if the account has late payments, or the primary holder maxes out the card. You can have it removed from your credit just as easily as it can be added.

4. Apply for and Open New Credit Accounts Only as Needed

Do not open accounts solely to obtain a better credit mix—it probably will not improve your credit score.

Unnecessary credit can harm credit scores in multiple ways, from creating too many hard inquiries on your credit report to overspending. These activities result in accumulated debt.

5. Don't Close Unused Credit Cards

Keeping unused credit cards open—if they are not costing you money in annual fees—is a smart strategy, because closing an account may increase your credit utilization ratio. Owing the same amount but having fewer open accounts may lower your credit scores.

6. Don't Apply for Too Much New Credit, Resulting in Multiple Inquiries

Opening a new credit card can increase your overall credit limit but applying for credit creates a hard inquiry on credit reports. Too many hard inquiries can negatively impact credit scores, though this effect will fade over time. Hard inquiries remain on credit reports for two years.

7. Dispute Any Inaccuracies on Your Credit Reports

You should check credit reports with the major credit reporting bureaus (**TransUnion, Equifax, and Experian**) for any inaccuracies. Additionally, there are other credit bureaus that sell your information to the major bureaus such **as LexisNexis, Credco and CoreLogic**. You can request a free copy of your credit file from these companies each year and they are responsible for adhering to the FCRA laws.

Incorrect information on your credit reports could drag your scores down. Verify that the accounts listed are correct. If you see errors, dispute the information and correct them right away. Monitoring your credit on a regular basis can help identify inaccuracies for timely correction, preventing lower scores.

THE POWER OF CREDIT CARD USAGE

Credit cards are great credit building tools when used responsibly. However, it is important to manage utilization, because credit cards can also be a route to debt if they are misused. Here are four ways you can build credit with a credit card:

> **Open your first credit card account.** If you have already established some credit history, look for a card with a low spending limit, which may be easier to qualify for if your credit history is limited. Make small charges that you can easily pay off right away and pay the balance down to at least 35% of the credit limit every month. This will help build a profile on your credit report of responsible credit use and reliable payment history.

> **Get a secured credit card.** If you have a minimum credit history or negative history, it may be difficult to get a regular credit card. A secured credit card may be an option. Secured credit cards are usually tied to a savings account, and the limit on the card is typically the amount

in the account or a percentage of the balance. Remarkably like a regular credit card, you build credit with a secured card by making responsible charges, keeping your balance low or at zero, and paying on time every month. Not all lenders report secured credit cards to the credit reporting companies, but the lender may be willing to convert the account to a traditional credit card after a certain period. You should ask these questions prior to deciding whether to open any account.

> **Open a joint account or become an authorized user.** If you're having trouble getting your own credit card, another option for building credit is to become an authorized user on someone else's account or open a joint account with someone who has a good credit history. Parents may choose to help establish credit for their kids by adding them to existing credit card accounts as an authorized user or opening a new card jointly. Adding an authorized user to an older account has the most impact on credit scores. One thing to keep in mind when

considering adding someone as an authorized user; the credit scoring models will not place a significant weight in the calculation unless the primary is your spouse or family member. For joint accounts, you are responsible for repaying charges on the card in partnership with the account holder. If you do not repay money borrowed on a joint account, the joint cardholder is responsible, or both parties will experience negative impacts of late and missed payments. It's important to make sure the primary account holder is a responsible person that intends to pay on time and keep the account balance low. Otherwise, there is a good possibility that you will end up in an unfavorable situation.

> **Request a credit limit increase.** After you have paid down your debt and decreased your utilization rate, or if your credit is already in good standing, you may consider asking for a credit limit increase from the credit card provider. Credit utilization ratio is a comparison between the total amount of credit available versus the total amount used and it is an important factor in

credit scores. A credit utilization ratio of **30 percent** or less is often considered good by lenders and others; the lower the ratio, the better it is for your credit score. For example, if you have $1,000 of available credit, and only owe $200, your credit utilization ratio is **20 percent**. Increasing your available credit can lower your credit utilization ratio and positively impact your credit score if you are careful not to max out the new limit. The lower your utilization rate, the better your credit score. On the other hand, asking for a credit limit increase when you have high balances may not be the best approach. It may be difficult to get a provider to agree to increase your limit based on more debt risk if your spending is not managed properly. In turn, it would negatively impact your credit score.

How to Build Credit without a Credit Card

There are multiple financial instruments available to build credit beyond credit cards. Remember, a credit report is a snapshot of how well you manage what you owe. Whenever credit is used wisely, that information can be included in your credit report. Here are five ways to build credit without a credit card:

- ➤ **Pay student loans diligently.** If you have a college degree, it is more than likely you have some student loan debt. Student loans are reported to credit bureaus every month and it is critical to make payments on time while building credit.

- ➤ **Take out an auto installment loan.** Auto loans are among the easiest types of loans to obtain, although the interest rate and terms can vary depending on who underwrites the loan. If you plan to buy a vehicle, shop around for the best possible deal, secure the loan, and ensure the agreed payment is delivered on time each month. If you have trouble finding a loan, you may need a cosigner to share responsibility for the payments. Other types of installment loans that help build credit history are mortgage and personal loans.

- ➤ **Obtain a secured loan.** Banks and credit unions understand it is not always easy to build credit when you are starting out with little credit history or negative marks on your credit report. Some offer credit-builder loans, or passbook/CD loans—low-risk loans designed specifically to help you build credit. They work much the same way a secured credit card works; for a credit-builder loan, you deposit a certain amount into an interest-bearing bank account and then borrow against that amount. The deposit is your collateral, and you will pay interest at a higher rate than your deposit earns it. For passbook or CD loans, some banks allow you to use an existing bank account or certificate of deposit as collateral for the loan. Before you take the loan, confirm with the lender that your on-time payments will appear on your credit report.

- ➤ **Non-profit lending circles.** Organizations such as the Mission Asset Fund (MAF) and its non-profit partners have been gaining popularity and expanding across the nation by providing low-income borrowers a way to get financing while building credit. Organizations such as these can provide affordable loans and report positive payment history to the credit bureaus.

> **Ask for credit where credit is due.** Just because you have never had a loan or credit card does not mean you do not know about paying bills. If you reliably pay your rent and utilities on time, you have demonstrated good money management habits and can ask for credit because of a good track record. Rental payments and utility bills do not typically appear on a credit report unless you fail to pay, and the leasing company or service provider sends the delinquent amount to a collection agency or files suit against you to recover the past due amount. However, recently, some companies have taken steps to change the reporting process. Experian was the first to include positive rental payment information on credit reports. You can ask landlords to report positive payment history to the bureaus. Experian also offers an Extended View score, which incorporates information from public records and sources beyond credit reports

to give lenders a more complete picture of an individual's money and credit-management habits. If you are having trouble getting approved for an auto loan, you can ask the finance company to request an Extended View score from Experian.

Establishing Credit With No Credit History

It is possible to have no credit history at all, especially if you're young and encounter challenges when trying to open a credit card or obtain a loan. In addition to the strategies outlined above, you can try the following tactics.

How to Establish Credit and Credit Scores:

- Ask someone with established credit to co-sign a loan for you, open a joint credit card account or add you as an authorized user to an existing credit card account.

- Ask your landlord and utility companies to report your positive payment history to the credit bureaus.

- Ask potential creditors to request your Extended View score from Experian, or Vantage Score from all three major credit bureaus. These scores incorporate more sources of information to build a better picture of financial history.

CHAPTER 5

Maintaining A Good Credit Score

Credit Building Requires Commitment

Building credit is a long-term investment and there is no single thing you can do to make that happen immediately. Credit history will gradually build as you continually increase the number of on-time payments. Even improving credit takes time, where the fastest change of bringing all accounts current, can take 30—60 days to reflect on credit reports. The best way to build and improve credit is to do so steadily, by paying all your bills on time every month, managing your credit utilization ratio, and ensuring you have a good credit mix.

How Long Does It Take to Rebuild Credit Scores?

If you have negative information on your credit report, such as late payments, a public record item (e.g., bankruptcy) or too many inquiries, you should pay your bills and wait. Time is your ally in improving credit scores. There is no **quick fix** for bad credit scores!

The length of time it takes to rebuild credit history after a negative change depends on reasons behind the change. Most negative changes in credit scores are due to addition of negative elements such as a delinquency or collection account. These new elements will continue affecting credit scores until they reach a certain age.

- Delinquencies remain on the credit report for seven years.

- Most public record items remain on your credit report for seven years, although some bankruptcies may remain for 10 years.

- Inquiries remain on your report for two years.

Rebuilding credit and improving scores takes time; there are no shortcuts. Another way to start improving credit scores is exploring credit building strategies such as **Self lending** and **Credit Card Builders**.

CHAPTER 6

Avoid Damaging Pitfalls

HOW CHANGES AFFECT SCORES

One common question most consumers ask is how specific actions will affect a credit score. For example, will closing two revolving accounts improve your credit score? While this question may seem easy to answer, there are many factors to consider. Credit scores are based entirely on information found in credit reports. Any change to credit reports could adversely affect credit scores. Simply closing two accounts not only lowers the number of open revolving accounts, but it also decreases the total amount of available credit. This leads to higher utilization rates, also called **balance-to-limit ratio**.

One change can affect many items on a credit report. It is impossible to provide a completely accurate assessment of how one specific action will affect a person's credit score. Therefore, credit risk factors provided with your score are important. They identify elements from credit history with the greatest impact.

CREDIT MISTAKES TO AVOID

Some financial behaviors can undermine efforts to build credit, so it is important to know what to avoid. Here are four common mistakes:

Not understanding how much you can afford. In general, a 43% debt-to-income ratio should be taken into consideration when taking on additional debt. The debt-to-income ratio is all your monthly debt obligations divided by your gross monthly income. The **Consumer Financial Protection Bureau (CFPB)** states that evidence from mortgage loan studies suggests that consumers with higher ratios are more likely to have difficulty making monthly payments.

Not having a budget. A personal budget is a necessity for all aspects of money management. Knowing how much you are spending and saving every month can help you make better decisions about how to use credit and manage debt.

Failing to shop around for installment loans. Choosing an installment loan, such as an auto or mortgage loan, should be like any other buying decision. You should compare shops for the best possible deal. Comparison shopping can help you find the lowest available interest rates, fees and service charges. Lenders recognize this shopping behavior and credit scoring systems take this into consideration, as well as inquiries made in a short period of time.

Failing to protect yourself from fraud. Credit card companies take measures to reduce fraud and federal law protects consumers from some effects of credit fraud. However, it is important to take steps to protect yourself as well. Review credit statements every month and monitor your credit report. Take care of cards by carrying only the ones you need in your wallet. Shred statements and receipts that have your account number on them, as well as any unwanted credit offers you receive in the mail.

Applying for multiple credit cards in a short amount of time. Suddenly taking on a lot of potential new revolving debt is a strong sign of risk and could indicate that you may use more credit than you can repay. This could negatively impact your balance-to-limit ratio and increase the number of hard inquiries impacting your credit.

Credit can be a powerful tool to help achieve your financial goals. It is important to understand how it works, how to build your credit and how to ensure credit history always works for you!

WHAT YOU MIGHT NOT KNOW ABOUT CREDIT SCORES

Credit scoring involves complex calculations and the more you build confidence and establish controls, the faster you will increase your credit score. In addition to knowing important factors considered in credit scoring, it can be helpful to know a few other factors impacting credit reports and scores.

Negative information on credit reports can lower credit scores. Negative information remains on credit reports for a set period. For example, late payments appear for **seven years** from the date you first missed a payment. Paying off a collection account will not immediately remove it from a credit report! **Bankruptcies** can remain on reports for **seven to ten years**, depending on the type of bankruptcy. On the bright side, all **negative information** will eventually cycle off credit reports. In the meantime, focus on positive actions such as paying <u>all bills on time</u> to increase scores.

Any time you fail to repay a debt as originally agreed, it can **negatively** affect your credit. A **negative** impact of settlement is still less than a **negative** effect of not paying debt or declaring bankruptcy. As a result, if you settle the debt with the **original creditor (not collection agency),** make sure to get it in writing. In the settlement letter, make sure to request the creditor to remove **negative** account(s) from your credit report.

A **good credit score** can open many doors and maximize buying power. For instance, you can obtain great interest rates and terms for life insurance! Additionally, **telecom companies** might look at credit scores before leasing smartphones.

Considering how important credit scores impact overall financial well-being, it is wise to do everything possible to ensure scores are between **680-750**. Regularly checking credit reports and scores are essential to maintaining a great financial position. When monitoring credit score changes, always compare data in each credit report (**Experian, Equifax, TransUnion**) to identify variations impacting scores. For instance, **Experian** may report an account as **open with a zero balance** and **Equifax** reports the same account as closed with a balance of $1,000. The variation in data directly impacts what scores are generated for each Bureau. In this case, a dispute is needed. Each credit bureau receives information from the same source **(creditor)** and multiple variations of data reported for the same account indicates inaccurate reporting.

Experian Boost™ helps by giving credit for utility and mobile phone bills you are already paying. Those payments are not reflected within payment history unless reported through this type of service.

This service is completely free and might boost credit scores fast by using positive payment history. Other services such as credit repair may cost up to thousands of dollars without assurance of removing inaccuracies.

If you have a long history of effectively managing credit and making payments on time, it is more than likely you have a good credit score. If you have never used credit or have negative information on your credit report, you may be less likely to secure a loan or credit card. If you are approved for the secure loan or credit card, you may get less favorable rates.

Building credit takes time, so it is important to begin building your credit before it is needed.

CHAPTER 7

Understanding Credit Reports

Your credit report is a record of credit history over time. There are three major credit reporting agencies or credit bureaus: **Experian, Equifax, and Transunion**. Each provides its own credit report. (You can check your 3-bureau credit report.)

Your credit report will generally contain the following types of information:

Personal information: This will include your "vitals," such as your name (and any aliases or common misspellings that may have been reported by a creditor), social security number and any variations that may have been reported, birth date, current and previous addresses, and current and previous employers. It does not include information about marital status, bank account balances, income, education level, race, religious preferences, medical history, personal lifestyle, political preferences, friends, criminal record or any other information unrelated to credit.

Trade account information: Here, you will find a list of your open credit accounts, including the creditor's name, your account number, the amount you owe, your available credit limit or original loan amount, and whether you have paid on time and are currently on payments. You will also find data on closed accounts, including the payment history on those accounts and whether they were closed in good standing. Negative information on credit reports can include missed or late payments and charge-offs. Learn more about the types of negative information that can appear on your credit report.

Public Record Information: Credit reports also contain information from the courts, including bankruptcy filings. Public records can negatively impact your credit.

Credit inquiries: Your report will show hard inquiries based on actions you have taken, such as applying for credit or financing or because of a collection. Soft inquiries, on the other hand, are a result of actions taken by others, like companies making promotional offers of credit or your lender conducting periodic reviews of your existing credit accounts. Soft inquiries also occur when you check your own credit report or when you use credit monitoring services from companies like Experian. These inquiries do not impact your credit score.

If you are looking for ways to improve your credit, taking care of negative information can help. Dispute with the reporting agencies if you find any inaccurate information on your credit report, pay down high balances, and bring all accounts current if you've fallen behind on any payments.

CHAPTER 8

Overcoming Debt Collectors

WHY IS DEBT VALIDATION IMPORTANT VERSUS JUST PAYING IT OFF?

There are several reasons why consumers should exercise their rights to validate a debt prior to paying it, especially when it comes from a collection agency.

Outlined below are key points why validation is important before paying a debt collector:

- Debt collectors use a common strategy of sending letters appearing to be legitimate stating a debt is owed. Technology has made it easy to obtain information about a person and their financial data to generate a debt collection notice.

- Always check and make sure the debt is not paid with the original creditor. If the debt collector is claiming you owe a debt and you can't remember whether it was paid with the original creditor, request the debt collector to provide proof the account belongs to you. Sometimes, debt collectors will attempt to make money on old debts. Typically, when this occurs, the debt collector does not have original documentation proving you owe the debt. It is your right under the Fair Debt Collection Practice Act to obtain proof before paying a debt.

- Sending a debt validation helps ensure the collection agency has the authority to collect on the account. The best way to confirm the original creditor sold a debt to the debt collector is requesting supporting documents and an agreement exists with the original creditor. Keep in mind, you have a contract/agreement with the original creditor; not the debt collector or collection agency. If your contractual agreement does not include language associated with paying a 3rd party collection agency, you are not responsible for paying that debt with a collection agency. Your obligation and responsibility remain with the original creditor. There are circumstances that might be favorable if you settle the debt with a collection agency and request in writing for the account to be deleted from your credit file.

CHAPTER 9

Fair Debt Collection Practice Act

Benefits of knowing the Fair Debt Collection Practice Act are outlined below:

- The FDCPA restricts debt collectors from calling before 8am and after 9pm. If you have an Attorney, the debt collector is required to cease direct communication with you and address all concerns with your appointed Attorney.

- Debt collectors can only contact a 3rd party (relative, employer or friend) to obtain contact information. Any request for additional information is a violation under the FDCPA.

- Debt collectors are required to send consumers a letter with basic information on accounts within five days of initial contact. The letter should include the amount of debt, original creditor's name, and a summary of consumer rights. Debt collection companies cannot falsify the amount owed on a debt and intentionally report inaccurate credit information to credit reporting agencies.

- Debt collectors cannot threaten to garnish or sell your property.

CHAPTER 10

Disputing with Collection Agencies

Verbal versus Written Disputes

Verbal debt validation request isn't sufficient to protect a consumer under the FDCPA laws, therefore the preferable route is dispute in writing. Disputing in writing ensures you have documentation to build a case if legal actions are required. Validation letters should specifically state what is disputed—whether it is the entire amount or a portion of the debt. Dispute letters sent within 30 days of receiving a debt collector's original letter enforces the FDCPA guidelines that prohibits any calls or contact to collect the debt until written verification is received, supporting that the account belongs to you. Sending debt validation letters via certified mail with return receipt is the best way to show proof of the date sent and receipt of the letter by the debt collector.

DEBT COLLECTOR'S RESPONSE

If the debt collector fails to verify the debt by providing sufficient documentation, all attempts to collect the debt should cease. Additionally, if no response is received from the initial validation request, you can follow up with a second request or proceed with writing a letter to the Bureaus and demand the account to be removed based on unverifiable evidence provided by the collection company.

Send the Credit Bureaus a copy of the original debt validation letter sent to the collection agency and include a copy of the certified mail receipt as support to increase the chance of removing the account from your credit file. The Credit Bureaus have 30 days to respond after the receipt of the request. In the letter to the Credit Bureaus, include the reason for dispute and the action needed (immediately delete the account).

CHAPTER 11

Control of Your Financial Journey

A study conducted by the Federal Trade Commission shows one in five consumers discovered mistakes on at least one of their credit reports, resulting in a negative impact on their credit scores. As consumers, it is critical to check credit reports with the major credit bureaus for accuracy on a regular basis. Each of the major bureaus maintain millions of consumer files and the volumes of records opens the door to reporting errors.

The most common reason why credit reports reflect errors is related to incorrect information provided by data furnishers such as banks, creditors, or collection agencies. Even though misreporting information is not intentional, the impact on consumers' credit scores can be significant. The Bureaus have no way of knowing if information is reported incorrectly unless consumer's act and file disputes. Another common credit reporting error is mixing files together based on similar addresses and names.

Finally, the keys to successfully navigating your financial journey requires attention and action! Maximizing your buying power is directly impacted by credit scores and worth the effort to ensure the credit reporting agencies have accurate information in your files.